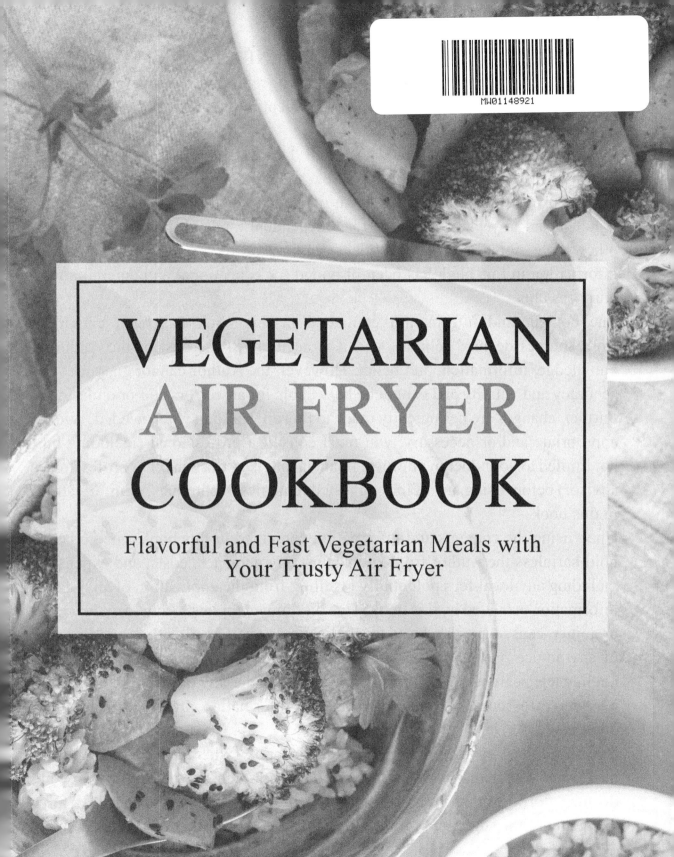

VEGETARIAN AIR FRYER COOKBOOK

Flavorful and Fast Vegetarian Meals with
Your Trusty Air Fryer

MW01148921

TEXT COPYRIGHT © HENRY IRVING

All rights reserved. No part of this guide may be reproduced in any form without permission in writing from the publisher except in the case of brief quotations embodied in critical articles or reviews.

LEGAL & DISCLAIMER

The information contained in this book and its contents is not designed to replace or take the place of any form of medical or professional advice; and is not meant to replace the need for independent medical, financial, legal, or other professional advice or services, as may be required. The content and information in this book has been provided for educational and entertainment purposes only.

The content and information contained in this book has been compiled from sources deemed reliable, and it is accurate to the best of the Author's knowledge, information, and belief. However, the Author cannot guarantee its accuracy and validity and cannot be held liable for any errors and/or omissions. Further, changes are periodically made to this book as and when needed. Where appropriate and/or necessary, you must consult a professional (including but not limited to your doctor, attorney, financial advisor, or such other professional advisor) before using any of the suggested remedies, techniques, or information in this book.

Upon using the contents and information contained in this book, you agree to hold harmless the Author from and against any damages, costs, and expenses, including any legal fees potentially resulting from the application of any of the information provided by this book. This disclaimer applies to any loss, damages or injury caused by the use and application, whether directly or indirectly, of any advice or information presented, whether for breach of contract, tort, negligence, personal injury, criminal intent, or under any other cause of action. You agree to accept all risks of using the information presented inside this book.

You agree that by continuing to read this book, where appropriate and/or necessary, you shall consult a professional (including but not limited to your doctor, attorney, or financial advisor or such other advisor as needed) before using any of the suggested remedies, techniques, or information in this book.

TABLE OF CONTENT

DESCRIPTION

In the quest for a healthy and satisfying diet, it can be difficult to find a balance between nutrition and flavor, especially when trying to lose weight. However, more and more people are turning to a vegetarian diet to achieve their health and environmental goals.

By adopting a vegetarian diet, individuals can improve their overall health and lower cholesterol levels. The reduction of animal protein in the diet also helps to detoxify the body and avoid chemical additives in processed foods and sugar. Moreover, vegetarianism benefits the environment by reducing deforestation and preserving natural resources.

«The Vegetarian Air Fryer Cookbook» is the ultimate guide to preparing healthy and delicious plant-based meals using air fryers. With over 50 easy-to-follow recipes, this book offers a wide range of tasty and nutritious options for vegetarians and anyone looking to add more plant-based meals to their diet. Air frying is a healthy and convenient way to prepare food, as it uses less oil than traditional frying methods while still achieving crispy and flavorful results. This book takes full advantage of this innovative cooking technique to create a variety of mouth-watering dishes that are both healthy and satisfying.

The book includes recipes for every meal of the day, from breakfast to dinner, and even snacks and desserts. You'll find classic favorites like French fries and onion rings, as well as more inventive ones.

Each recipe includes a detailed ingredient list, step-by-step instructions, and nutritional information, making it easy to plan and prepare healthy and tasty meals. In addition to the recipes, the book also offers practical tips for using and maintaining air fryers, as well as suggestions for how to incorporate more plant-based foods into your diet.

Whether you're a seasoned vegetarian or simply looking to incorporate more plant-based meals into your diet, «The Vegetarian Air Fryer Cookbook» is the ultimate resource for healthy and delicious air fryer recipes.

WHAT IS VEGETARIAN DIET?

A vegetarian diet is a dietary pattern that excludes the consumption of meat, poultry, seafood, and other animal-derived products. Vegetarians typically consume a variety of plant-based foods, such as fruits, vegetables, whole grains, legumes, nuts, and seeds.

There are several types of vegetarian diets, including lacto-ovo vegetarianism, which includes dairy products and eggs in addition to plant-based foods, and veganism, which excludes all animal-derived products, including dairy and eggs.

A vegetarian diet has been associated with numerous health benefits, such as lower risk of heart disease, type 2 diabetes, and some cancers, as well as improved digestion and weight management. Additionally, vegetarianism can also reduce the environmental impact of food production and support animal welfare.

It is important to note that a vegetarian diet can still be unhealthy if it is based on highly processed foods or lacks essential nutrients. Therefore, it is essential to consume a balanced variety of whole, nutrient-dense foods to meet daily nutritional needs when following a vegetarian diet.

A well-planned vegetarian diet can provide all the necessary nutrients that the body needs. However, some nutrients may be more difficult to obtain in a vegetarian diet, such as vitamin B12, iron, zinc, calcium, and omega-3 fatty acids. It is important for vegetarians to pay attention to these nutrients and ensure that they are getting enough through their diet or supplementation.

Plant-based sources of protein can be found in beans, lentils, chickpeas, nuts, seeds, tofu, tempeh, and seitan. Combining different plant-based protein sources throughout the day can help ensure that the body is getting all the essential amino acids it needs.

Iron can be found in leafy green vegetables, beans, fortified cereals, and grains. Zinc can be found in beans, nuts, whole grains, and fortified cereals. Calcium can be found in leafy green vegetables, fortified plant milks, and calcium-set tofu. Omega-3 fatty acids can be found in flaxseeds, chia seeds, hemp seeds, walnuts, and algae-based supplements.

Vegetarian diets can also be tailored to meet different health goals and preferences. For example, some vegetarians choose to consume dairy products and eggs for additional protein and nutrients, while others opt for a vegan diet for ethical or environmental reasons. Plant-based diets can also be low in fat or high in healthy fats, depending on the types of foods consumed.

Overall, a well-planned vegetarian diet can provide numerous health benefits and support environmental sustainability. It is important to consult a healthcare provider or registered dietitian to ensure that nutritional needs are being met when transitioning to a vegetarian diet.

There are several types of vegetarians, each with their own set of dietary restrictions and allowances. Here are some of the most common types of vegetarians:

Lacto-ovo vegetarian: This is the most common type of vegetarian.

Lacto-ovo vegetarians exclude meat, poultry, and fish from their diet, but they include dairy products (lacto) and eggs (ovo).

Lacto vegetarian: Lacto vegetarians exclude meat, poultry, fish, and eggs from their diet, but they include dairy products.

Ovo vegetarian: Ovo vegetarians exclude meat, poultry, fish, and dairy products from their diet, but they include eggs.

Vegan: Vegans exclude all animal-derived products from their diet, including meat, poultry, fish, dairy, eggs, and honey. They also avoid products made from animals, such as leather, wool, and silk.

Pescatarian: Pescatarians exclude meat and poultry from their diet, but they include fish and seafood.

Flexitarian: Flexitarians follow a mostly vegetarian diet, but they occasionally eat meat or fish.

Raw food vegetarian: Raw food vegetarians consume only uncooked and unprocessed plant-based foods.

Overall, it's important for individuals to choose the type of vegetarianism that best aligns with their ethical beliefs, personal preferences, and nutritional needs. Consulting with a registered dietitian can help ensure that a vegetarian diet is nutritionally adequate and sustainable.

WHY YOU NEED TO START THE VEGETARIAN DIET?

I want to tell you about how a plant-based diet can improve your health and lifestyle. If you compare two people, one a meat-eater and the other a vegetarian, the vegetarian tends to consume less saturated, overweight foods and cholesterol-raising foods. The vegetarian also gets more vitamins, as well as folic acid, potassium, dietary fiber, magnesium, and phytochemicals, among others. Thanks to the Vegetarian diet, vegetarians are more likely to have lower cholesterol and blood pressure levels as well as lower BMI (Body Mass Index). These three measures are associated with the risk of chronic disease as well as longevity.

However, it is important to note that eating healthy plant foods is not the only thing that will allow you to live a healthy lifestyle. It is also very important to exercise regularly, lives a stress-free life, quit smoking and drinking, and be psychologically healthy.

Adopting whole foods, plant-based diet will not only benefit your waistline but can also reduce the risk and symptoms of some chronic diseases. Here's what we know from medical research to date:

Diabetes

Because it focuses on fresh ingredients and it packs plenty of vitamins, antioxidants, and minerals, this diet is a great way to keep your diabetes under control. This lifestyle controls excess insulin, which in turn lowers our blood sugar levels.

Regulating blood sugar levels is vastly important to living a healthier lifestyle. There is a need for balancing a lot of whole foods into this plan to find quality sources of protein and consume carbs that are low in sugar. That makes the body burn fat much more efficiently, and you will have more energy as a result. In short, a natural diet with fresh produce is a natural combater of diabetes.

Heart Disease

Vegetarians have a lower risk of cardiac diseases (mainly heart attacks) and death from heart failures. Eating more plant-based foods through a Vegetarian diet may reduce one's risk for cardiovascular disease. Research has shown that a diet comprised predominantly of plant-based foods, such as fruits, vegetables, legumes, and nuts is associated with a lower risk of CVD. If you want to keep your heart in good health, the best thing is to eat whole-grain foods and legumes (high in fiber). Such foods keep the blood sugar levels in balance and reduce the levels of cholesterol.

Cancer

Vegetarian diet patterns have been associated with reduced risk of certain types of cancer, including colon cancer. According to the Oxford Vegetarian Study and EPIC-Oxford, fish-eaters had a lower risk of certain cancers than vegetarians who don't consume fish at all.

Enhance Your Mood

The diet can help you to be positive, even when things aren't going your way. Healthy living does that. When you have eaten enough food to fuel you with lots of nutrients, your body notices. Fulfillment and productivity enhance your mood. For one, applying the diet correctly will make you feel like you're doing something good for yourself and thus enhances your overall mood.

Weight Management

Although the main focus of this diet is not weight loss, it will surely help with it if that's what you're looking for. Just look at it from this point of view: fresh, clean food combined with whole grains, good fats, less sugar, and plenty of liquids coupled with copious amounts of exercise. By transitioning to healthy foods and a healthy lifestyle, you'll shed pounds without causing drastic imbalances in your body. Also, it is known that plant-based diets like the Vegetarian diet are really helpful in losing weight. The mere fact that you stopped eating junk food and processed food with sugar and unhealthy fats is already a very good start to weight loss!

Improve Skin Condition

Fish have Omega-3 fatty acids. They strengthen the skin membrane and make it more elastic and firmer. Olive oil, red wine, and tomatoes contain a lot of antioxidants to protect against skin damage brought about by chemical reactions and prolonged sun exposure.

Boost Brain Power

The Vegetarian diet can also counteract the brain's poor ability to perform. Choosing this lifestyle will actually help you preserve your memory, leading to an overall increase in your cognitive health.

Normally cognitive disorders are caused by a scenario where your brain is unable to get a sufficient amount of dopamine.

Dopamine is a compound or chemical present in the brain responsible for passing information from one neuron to the other. It is responsible for thought processing, mood regulation, and proper body movements.

The ability of this diet to help boost your cognitive health is normally linked to the combination of its anti-inflammatory fruits and vegetables, its healthy fats, and nuts.

These foods normally battle cognitive decline that is caused by age. But how do these foods do it? These foods normally deal with elements that cause impaired brain function like inflammation, free radicals, and exposure to toxicity.

Fatty fish, nuts, and olive oils all contain omega-3 fatty acids that usually help reduce the level of inflammation in your body. Such vegetables like spinach, kale, and broccoli that are dark green contain vitamin E, which is known to protect your body from an anti-inflammatory molecule known as cytokines.

Vegetables like spinach, broccoli, and fruits like raspberries, cherries, and watermelon all have antioxidants that neutralize free radicals that affect your brain. The Vegetarian diet also tends to focus on monounsaturated fats, which come from oils like olive oil. The oils and the fatty acids that you get from omega 3 (from fish) combine to keep your arteries unblocked.

That automatically increases the health of your brain and reduces your risk of getting diseases like Alzheimer's disease and dementia.

USEFUL TIPS ON HOW TO SWITCH TO A VEGETARIAN DIET

Switching to a vegetarian diet can be a big lifestyle change, but it can also be a very rewarding one for your health and the environment. Here are some useful tips on how to make the transition to a vegetarian diet:

Start slowly: Gradually reducing your intake of meat and animal products can make the transition to a vegetarian diet more manageable.

Experiment with new foods: Vegetarian diets can be very diverse, with a wide variety of fruits, vegetables, whole grains, and legumes available. Try incorporating new ingredients and recipes into your meals to discover new favorites.

Find vegetarian substitutes: Many vegetarian substitutes for meat and dairy products are available in grocery stores, such as plant-based meats, tofu, tempeh, and dairy-free milk and cheese alternatives.

Educate yourself: Research the health benefits and environmental impact of a vegetarian diet to stay motivated and informed.

Plan your meals: Planning your meals and snacks in advance can help you make sure that you are getting all the necessary nutrients in your diet. Consider consulting with a registered dietitian to help you plan a balanced vegetarian diet.

Be patient and persistent: Changing your eating habits takes time, so be patient with yourself and celebrate your successes along the way.

FOODS TO EAT AND AVOID

Foods to eat:

- Fruits: such as apples, bananas, oranges, berries, etc.

- Vegetables: such as leafy greens, broccoli, carrots, tomatoes, etc.

- Legumes: such as lentils, chickpeas, black beans, kidney beans, etc.

- Whole grains: such as brown rice, quinoa, oats, barley, etc.

- Nuts and seeds: such as almonds, walnuts, chia seeds, flax seeds, etc.

- Dairy products (for lacto-ovo vegetarians): such as milk, cheese, etc.

- Eggs (for ovo-vegetarians and lacto-ovo vegetarians)

Foods to limit or avoid:

- Meat: such as beef, pork, chicken, turkey, etc.

- Seafood: such as fish, shrimp, crab, etc.

- Animal-based fats: such as lard, butter, etc.

- Refined carbohydrates: such as white bread, white rice, pasta, etc.

- Highly processed foods: such as sugary snacks, chips, etc.

23

It is important to note, if you are a flexitarian, your consumption of chicken or fish is not restricted. Feel your body, if you feel like eating a piece of salmon, don't deny yourself. Since fish and seafood are high in omega-3 fats, I recommend eating fish at least 2 times a week to get your nutrients.

WILL THIS DIET HELP YOU LOSE WEIGHT?

The average person on a vegetarian diet may weigh less than those who regularly eat meat and animal products. This is due to the high protein and low-fat content of animal products.

Losing weight is an important motivator for many people when transitioning to a new diet. Not only does it make them feel better, but it can also improve their health.

Plant-based diets tend to be less caloric and rich in protein, which makes them great for weight loss. People who follow these diets can also have lower cholesterol levels because of their higher fiber content; this makes them great for treating obesity and other conditions associated with excessive blood cholesterol levels.

It's no coincidence that obesity is increasing at the same time that highly processed foods have become available. Processed foods can slow weight loss in several ways.

For instance, a diet of processed foods that don't provide enough iron could affect your ability to exercise, since iron is required to move oxygen around your body. This would limit your ability to burn calories through exercise.

Low-nutrient diets can also interfere with weight loss because people feel less fatigued after eating.

One study of 786 participants compared the fatness of participants who followed a low-nutrient diet to a high-nutrient diet.

After following the high micronutrient diet, about 80% of the participants felt more obese, even though they consumed fewer calories than the low micronutrient diet.

When trying to increase your nutrient intake, it is best to eat real foods, which contain many nutrients such as minerals, vitamins, and minerals that are not easily obtained from supplements.

Moreover, the nutrients in whole foods interact better with each other and are absorbed better than in supplements.

26

If you are interested in applying the Vegetarian diet to your life to lose weight, then these general dieting tips paired with this diet eating habits will help you maximize your weight loss.

Eat Slowly

It takes twenty minutes for your food to start digesting and give you a feeling of fullness after you eat a meal. Therefore, slow down and chew your food so that you can actually taste it and enjoy the flavor. If you tend to eat fast, you may find that you eat more because it takes that twenty minutes to get your internal system fired up.

Drink Water Before Your Meal

Try drinking a full eight-ounce glass of water before you sit down to eat a meal. Sometimes thirst can be mistaken for a feeling of hunger. Drinking a glass of water before you eat can get the digestion process started quicker, which can cause you to eat less during a meal.

Exercise

Adhere to the most foundational level, which is a daily activity. Do your best to get thirty minutes of exercise every day.

Adapt to Using Healthy Oil

When on a Vegetarian diet, fats are very important. But ensure you are ingesting the correct ones by using natural oils instead of butter.

Change the Way You Think About Food

See vegetables and fruits as snacks. Slice your vegetables into ready-to-eat snack sizes and wash your fruits when you bring them home from the store so that they are ready to grab as a quick snack when you're feeling hungry.

Always have a jar of mixed nuts within your reach on the kitchen counter and eat a handful of those along with your vegetable or fruit snack.

Prepackaged Snacks

Prepackaged snacks into portion sizes rather than eating from the full container. This can prevent overeating.

When you pre-allocate how much of a snack you're going to eat, then you're helping yourself stay disciplined.

Snack Two or Three Times a Day

Enjoy two or three snacking times a day where you eat a serving of fruit or vegetables with no salt or sugar added. Schedule a snack in the morning, afternoon, and before bed.

Learn a Well-Balanced Eating Plan

The longer you adhere to the Vegetarian diet, the more energy and vitality you will receive.

The Vegetarian diet offers a well-balanced eating plan that includes the correct amount of each food group.

AIR FRYER & HOW IT WORKS?

Air Fryer is a kitchen appliance with versatility and ingenious design that uses patented technology to cook food with superheated air. It heats up within a minute, and there is a swift flow of hot air within the dedicated chamber, making food cook evenly while using less oil. This game-changing kitchen appliance has rapid air circulation technology, which enables hot air to surround the food you want to cook at high speeds to develop the crispy food we all crave for. On top of the delicious crunchy food, little oil is used in the process, making it a guilt-free delicacy!

Here are some tips for preparing healthy foods in an air fryer:

Vegetables are some of the easiest foods to cook in an air fryer. A wide variety of plants can be cooked, from delicate beans to root vegetables. For the best cooking experience, soak the vegetables, especially the harder ones, in cold water for 15-20 minutes. Then, dry them using a clean kitchen towel.

Roasting with air is a new cooking trend that you have to try because you can finally prepare your winter favorites.

Flip foods when half of the cooking time is attained. Just as you would if you were cooking on a grill or in a skillet, you need to turn foods over so that they brown evenly.

You can bake your favorite recipes in your air fryer, but always check with the machine's manual before using new baking ware with the air fryer.

Aim at cooking your food to the desired doneness because the recipes are flexible, and they are designed for all air fryer models. If you feel that the food needs more cooking time, then adjust it and cook for a few more minutes. It is not necessary to stick to a recipe time, as certain ingredients can vary in size and firmness from one place to another.

When it comes to cooking time, it changes depending on the particular air fryer model, the size of the food, food pre-preparation, and so on. For shorter cooking cycles, you should preheat the air fryer for about 3-4 minutes. Otherwise, if you put the ingredients into the cold cooking basket, the cooking time needs to be increased by 3 additional minutes.

Use a good quality oil spray to brush food and cooking baskets; it is also helpful for easy cleanup.

BREAKFAST
RECIPES

AIR BREAD

 Cooking Difficulty: 3/10

 Cooking Time: 28 minutes

 Servings: 19

INGREDIENTS

- 3 eggs
- 1 tsp. baking powder
- ¼ tsp. sea salt
- 1 c. almond flour
- ¼ c. vegan butter

DESCRIPTION

STEP 1

Soften the butter to room temperature. Whisk the eggs with a hand mixer. Combine the two and add the rest of the fixings to make a dough.

STEP 2

Knead the dough and cover with a tea towel for about 10 minutes.

STEP 3

Set the Air Fryer at 350°F. Air fry the bread for 15 minutes.

STEP 5

Remove the bread and let it cool down on a wooden board. Slice and serve with your favorite meal or as it is.

NUTRITIONAL INFORMATION

40 Calories, 3.9g Fat, 0.2g Carbs, 1g Protein

AVOCADO MUFFINS

 Cooking Difficulty: 3/10	Cooking Time: 13 minutes	Servings: 7

NUTRITIONAL INFORMATION

133 Calories, 12.4g Fat, 2.9g Carbs, 2.2g Protein

INGREDIENTS

- 1 c. almond flour
- ½ tsp. baking soda
- 1 tsp. apple cider vinegar
- 1 egg
- 4 tbsps. vegan butter
- 3 scoops stevia powder
- ½ c. pitted avocado
- 1 oz. melted dark chocolate

DESCRIPTION

STEP 1
Preheat the Air Fryer to 355°F.

STEP 2
Whisk the almond flour, baking soda, and vinegar. Add the stevia powder and melted chocolate.

STEP 3
Whisk the egg in another container and add to the mixture along with the butter.

STEP 4
Peel, cube, and mash the avocado and add. Blend with a hand mixer to make the flour mixture smooth. Pour into the muffin forms (½ full). Cook for 9 minutes.

STEP 5
Lower the heat (340°F) and cook for 3 more minutes.

STEP 6
Chill before serving for the best results.

AVOCADO EGG BOATS

 Cooking Difficulty: 2/10	Cooking Time: 8 minutes	Servings: 2

INGREDIENTS

- 1 avocado
- 2 eggs
- chopped chives
- chopped parsley
- pepper
- salt

DESCRIPTION

STEP 1
Warm up the fryer to 350°F.

STEP 2
Remove the pit from the avocado. Slice and scoop out part of the flesh. Shake with the seasonings.

STEP 3
Add an egg to each half and place in the preheated Air Fryer for 6 minutes.

STEP 4
Remove and serve with some additional parsley and chives if desired.

NUTRITIONAL INFORMATION

288 Calories, 26.4g Fat, 7.5g Carbs, 7g Protein

MUSHROOM, ONION, & CHEESE FRITTATA

 Cooking Difficulty: 2/10

 Cooking Time: 16 minutes

 Servings: 7

NUTRITIONAL INFORMATION

284 Calories, 22g Fat, 6g Carbs, 7g Protein

INGREDIENTS

- 1 tbsp. olive oil
- 2 c. sliced mushrooms
- 1 small sliced onion
- 3 eggs
- ½ c. grated vegan cheese
- salt

DESCRIPTION

STEP 1
Program the Air Fryer to 320°F.

STEP 2
Warm up a skillet (medium heat) and add the oil.

STEP 3
Toss in the mushrooms and onions and sauté for about 5 minutes. Add to the Air Fryer.

STEP 4
Whisk the eggs with the salt and dump on top of the fixings in the fryer.

STEP 5
Sprinkle with the cheese and air fry for 10 minutes.

STEP 6
Take right out of the basket and serve. Yummy!

EGGS IN A ZUCCHINI NEST

 Cooking Difficulty:
2/10

 Cooking Time:
11 minutes

 Servings:
4

INGREDIENTS

- 8 oz. grated zucchini
- avocado oil
- ¼ tsp. sea salt
- ½ tsp. black pepper
- ½ tsp. paprika
- 4 eggs
- 4 ramekins

DESCRIPTION

STEP 1
Preheat the Air Fryer at 356ºF.

STEP 2
Grate the zucchini. Add the oil to the ramekins and add the zucchini in a nest shape. Sprinkle with the paprika, salt, and pepper.

STEP 3
Whisk the eggs and add to the nest.

STEP 4
Air fry for 7 minutes. Chill for 3 minutes and serve in the ramekin.

NUTRITIONAL INFORMATION

221 Calories, 18g Fat, 2g Carbs, 7g Protein

BLUEBERRY MUFFINS

 Cooking Difficulty: 2/10

 Cooking Time: 22 minutes

 Servings: 2

INGREDIENTS

- 1 cup all-purpose flour
- 1/2 cup rolled oats
- 1/4 cup granulated sugar
- 1 tsp baking powder
- 1/2 tsp baking soda
- 1/4 tsp salt
- 1/4 cup unsweetened applesauce
- 1/4 cup vegan milk
- 1 tsp vanilla extract
- 1 cup fresh or frozen blueberries

NUTRITIONAL INFORMATION

Calories: 215, Fat: 12.9g, Carbs: 8.5g, Protein: 14.2g

DESCRIPTION

STEP 1
Preheat your air fryer to 350°F.

STEP 2
In a mixing bowl, whisk together all-purpose flour, rolled oats, granulated sugar, baking powder, baking soda, and salt.

STEP 3
In another bowl, mix together unsweetened applesauce, almond milk, and vanilla extract until well combined.

STEP 4
Gradually stir in the flour mixture into the applesauce mixture until well combined. Gently fold in the blueberries into the muffin mixture.

STEP 5
Spray the muffin cups of your air fryer basket with non-stick cooking spray or oil. Spoon the muffin mixture into the muffin cups, filling them about 2/3 full.

STEP 6
Cook the muffins in the air fryer for 12-15 minutes or until a toothpick inserted into the center comes out clean.

STEP 7
Use a spatula to carefully remove the muffins from the air fryer basket. Allow the muffins to cool in the muffin cups for a few minutes, then remove them from the cups and transfer them to a cooling rack to cool completely.

STEP 8
Serve.

CRAVING CINNAMON TOAST

 Cooking Difficulty: 1/10

 Cooking Time: 6 minutes

 Servings: 3

INGREDIENTS

- 6 slices bread
- ½ c. sugar
- 1 stick vegan butter
- 1½ tsps. vanilla extract
- 1½ tsps. cinnamon

DESCRIPTION

STEP 1
Preheat your Air Fryer up to 400 degrees F.

STEP 2
In a microwave-proof bowl, mix butter, sugar, and vanilla extract. Warm the mixture for 30 seconds until everything melts as you stir.

STEP 3
Pour the mixture over bread slices. Lay the bread slices in your air fryer's cooking basket and cook for 5 minutes.

STEP 4
Serve with fresh banana and berry sauce. Enjoy!

NUTRITIONAL INFORMATION

Calories: 217, Fat: 12.5g, Carbs: 4.7g, Protein: 18.8g

PEACHES AND CREAM

 Cooking Difficulty: 2/10	Cooking Time: 20 minutes	Servings: 3

NUTRITIONAL INFORMATION

Calories 338, Fat 29.2g, Carbs 21g, Protein 4.2g

INGREDIENTS

- 6 ripe peaches
- 1 cup coconut cream
- 1 tsp vanilla extract
- Cooking spray

DESCRIPTION

STEP 1
Preheat the air fryer to 375°F..Cut the peaches in half and remove the pit. Spray the air fryer basket with cooking spray and place the peach cut side up in the basket.

STEP 2
Cook the peaches in the air fryer for 5-6 minutes, or until they are tender and slightly caramelized.

STEP 3
While the peaches are cooking, in a mixing bowl, whip the coconut cream and vanilla extract together until the cream forms stiff peaks.

STEP 4
Once the peaches are cooked, remove them from the air fryer and place them on a serving platter or individual plates.

STEP 5
Spoon a dollop of the whipped cream onto each peach half. Serve the Peaches and Cream immediately, while the peaches are still warm. Enjoy!

HERBED SWEET POTATO HASH

 Cooking Difficulty: 3/10

 Cooking Time: 20 minutes

 Servings: 5

INGREDIENTS

- 4 sweet potatoes, peeled and diced
- 1 c. sliced button mushrooms
- 1 chopped onion
- ½ chopped green bell pepper
- 2 tbsps. lemon juice
- 2 tbsps. olive oil
- ½ tsp. rosemary, dried
- salt, and pepper

DESCRIPTION

STEP 1
Preheat Air Fryer to 360°F.

STEP 2
In a mixing bowl, mix together all ingredients. Season with salt and pepper.

STEP 3
Take out Air Fryer cooking basket, and then place sweet potato mixture.

STEP 4
Cook for about 25-30 minutes.

STEP 5
Serve and enjoy!

NUTRITIONAL INFORMATION

Calories: 203, Fat: 6.5g, Carbs: 36.2g, Protein: 3.4g

BLUEBERRY PANCAKES

 Cooking Difficulty: 2/10	Cooking Time: 24 minutes	Servings: 2

INGREDIENTS

- 1 cup all-purpose flour
- 2 tbsp granulated sugar
- 2 tsp baking powder
- 1/4 tsp salt
- 1 cup non-dairy milk (such as almond, soy, or oat milk)
- 1 tbsp apple cider vinegar
- 2 tbsp coconut oil, melted
- 1/2 tsp vanilla extract
- 1/2 cup fresh blueberries
- Non-stick cooking spray or oil, for frying

NUTRITIONAL INFORMATION

Calories: 215, Fat: 12.9g, Carbs: 8.5g, Protein: 14.2g

DESCRIPTION

STEP 1

Preheat the deep fryer to 375°F (190°C). In a mixing bowl, whisk together the flour, sugar, baking powder, and salt until well combined.

STEP 2

In a separate bowl, mix together the non-dairy milk and apple cider vinegar. Let it sit for 2-3 minutes to curdle.

STEP 3

Add the melted coconut oil and vanilla extract to the milk mixture and stir to combine.

STEP 4

Pour the wet ingredients into the dry ingredients and stir until just combined. Do not overmix. Gently fold in the blueberries. Spray the deep fryer basket with non-stick cooking spray or brush with oil.

STEP 5

Using a 1/4 cup measuring cup, scoop the pancake batter and pour it into the deep fryer basket. Repeat until the basket is full, but do not overcrowd the basket.

STEP 6

Close the lid and cook for 5-7 minutes, or until the pancakes are golden brown and cooked through. Repeat with the remaining batter, making sure to spray the basket with non-stick cooking spray or oil between batches.

STEP 7

Serve the pancakes warm with your favorite toppings, such as maple syrup, vegan butter, or more fresh blueberries.

EGG BUTTER

 Cooking Difficulty: 2/10	Cooking Time: 18 minutes	Servings: 4

INGREDIENTS

- 4 eggs
- 1 tsp. salt
- 4 tbsps. vegan butter

DESCRIPTION

STEP 1
Add a layer of foil to the Air Fryer basket and add the eggs. Cook at 320°F for 17 minutes. Transfer to an ice-cold water bath to chill.

STEP 2
Peel and chop the eggs and combine with the rest of the fixings. Combine well until it achieves a creamy texture.

STEP 3
Enjoy with your Air Fried Bread.

NUTRITIONAL INFORMATION

164 Calories, 8g Fat, 2.6g Carbs, 3g Protein

VEGAN AIR FRYER SPINACH PANCAKES

Cooking Difficulty: 2/10	Cooking Time: 25 minutes	Servings: 4

INGREDIENTS

- 1 cup all-purpose flour
- 1 tsp baking powder
- 1/4 tsp salt
- 1/4 tsp black pepper
- 1/4 tsp garlic powder
- 1/4 tsp onion powder
- 1/2 cup almond milk (or other non-dairy milk)
- 1 tbsp apple cider vinegar
- 2 tbsp olive oil
- 2 cups fresh spinach, chopped

NUTRITIONAL INFORMATION

Calories: 222; Fat: 1.2g; Carbs: 8.4g; Protein: 4g

DESCRIPTION

STEP 1
Preheat your air fryer to 350°F.

STEP 2
In a mixing bowl, whisk together flour, baking powder, salt, black pepper, garlic powder, and onion powder.

STEP 3
In another bowl, mix together the almond milk and apple cider vinegar, and let it sit for a few minutes to curdle. Gradually stir in the flour mixture into the almond milk mixture until well combined.

STEP 4
Add the chopped spinach and mix until evenly distributed.

STEP 5
Brush the air fryer basket with olive oil. Spoon the pancake mixture onto the basket, forming about 2-inch diameter pancakes.

STEP 6
Brush the top of the pancakes with olive oil. Cook the pancakes in the air fryer for 8-10 minutes or until the edges are golden brown and the pancakes are cooked through.

STEP 7
Use a spatula to carefully remove the pancakes from the air fryer basket.

STEP 8
Serve the spinach pancakes warm with your favorite toppings, such as vegan sour cream, chives, or salsa.

SPINACH MUFFINS

 Cooking Difficulty: 2/10	Cooking Time: 22 minutes	Servings: 4

INGREDIENTS

- 2¼ c. spinach
- 4 tsps. vegan milk
- 1 tbsp. olive oil
- 4 large eggs
- salt
  pepper
- 4 ramekins
- red bell peper (optional)

DESCRIPTION

STEP 1
Set the fryer temperature to 356°F. Spray the ramekins.

STEP 2
Warm up the oil in a skillet (medium heat) and sauté the spinach until wilted. Drain.

STEP 3
Divide the spinach and rest of the fixings in each of the ramekins.

STEP 4
Sprinkle with the salt and pepper. Bake until set (20 minutes).Serve when they are to your liking.

NUTRITIONAL INFORMATION

190 Calories, 13g Fat, 2g Carbs, 5g Protein

TENDER POTATO PANCAKES

Cooking Difficulty: 3/10	Cooking Time: 15 minutes	Servings: 4

INGREDIENTS

- 4 potatoes, peeled and cleaned
- 1 chopped onion
- 1 beaten egg
- ¼ c. almod milk
- 2 tbsps. vegan butter
- ½ tsp. garlic powder
- ¼ tsp. salt
- 3 tbsps. all-purpose flour
- pepper

NUTRITIONAL INFORMATION

Calories: 248, Fat: 11g, Carbs: 33g, Protein: 6g

DESCRIPTION

STEP 1
Peel your potatoes and shred them up.

STEP 2
Soak the shredded potatoes under cold water to remove starch.

STEP 3
Drain the potatoes.

STEP 4
Take a bowl and add eggs, milk, butter, garlic powder, salt, and pepper.

STEP 5
Add in flour.

STEP 6
Mix well.

STEP 7
Add the shredded potatoes.

STEP 8
Pre-heat your air fryer to 390 degrees F.

STEP 9
Add ¼ cup of the potato pancake batter to your cooking basket and cook for 12 minutes until the golden brown texture is seen.

STEP 10
Enjoy!

AIR FRYER BAKED EGGS

 Cooking Difficulty: 2/10

 Cooking Time: 8 minutes

 Servings: 2

INGREDIENTS

- 2 eggs
- 2 tbsps. almod milk
- 1 chopped tomato
- salt and pepper
- parsley, chopped

DESCRIPTION

STEP 1
Pre-heat your oven to 180 degrees F. Dice tomatoes and add them to the ramekins.

STEP 2
Add a tablespoon of milk onto each ramekin.

STEP 3
Crack an egg into each ramekin. Season both with salt and pepper.

STEP 4
Place ramekins into Air Fryer cooking basket and cook for 7 minutes.

STEP 5
Serve with a garnish of parsley and enjoy!

NUTRITIONAL INFORMATION

Calories: 215, Fat: 12.9g, Carbs: 8.5g, Protein: 14.2g

MAIN RECIPES

AIR FRYER PUMPKIN SLICES

 Cooking Difficulty: 1/10	 Cooking Time: 12 minutes	Servings: 4

INGREDIENTS

- 1 medium pumpkin, sliced into 1/2 inch rounds
- 2 tablespoons olive oil
- 1 teaspoon salt
- 1/2 teaspoon black pepper
- 1/4 teaspoon garlic powder
- cooking spray

DESCRIPTION

STEP 1

Preheat the air fryer to 375°F for 5 minutes. In a mixing bowl, combine the olive oil, salt, black pepper, and garlic powder.

STEP 2

Brush both sides of each pumpkin slice with the spice mixture. Spray the air fryer basket with cooking spray.

STEP 3

Arrange the pumpkin slices in a single layer in the air fryer basket. Cook for 8-10 minutes, flipping the slices halfway through until they are tender and lightly browned. Serve immediately with your favorite vegetables and nuts.

NUTRITIONAL INFORMATION

Calories 73, Fat 5g, Carbs 7g, Protein 1g

DIJON AND LEMON ARTICHOKES

 Cooking Difficulty: 3/10	Cooking Time: 28 minutes	Servings: 4

NUTRITIONAL INFORMATION

108 Calories, 7.5g Fat, 2.4g Carbs, 3.1g Protein

INGREDIENTS

- 2 artichokes
- 1 lemon
- ¼ tsp. salt
- ¼ tsp. pepper
- 2 tbsps. dijon mustard
- 2 tbsps. olive oil
- 1 lemon wedge

DESCRIPTION

STEP 1

Cut the stem off the artichoke and remove the tough outer leaves. Using kitchen shears, trim the top of the artichoke and snip off the pointy tips of the remaining leaves. Cut the artichoke in half lengthwise and use a spoon to scoop out the fuzzy choke in the center.

STEP 2

In a small mixing bowl, combine garlic, olive oil, salt, dijon mustard, and pepper. Brush the mixture over the artichoke halves, making sure to coat all surfaces.

STEP 3

Preheat the air fryer to 375°F. Place the artichoke halves in the air fryer basket, cut side down.

STEP 4

Cook the artichoke for 15-20 minutes or until the leaves are tender and the edges are crispy.

STEP 5

Remove the artichoke from the air fryer basket and serve with lemon wedges. Enjoy!

GRILLED EGGPLANT

 Cooking Difficulty: 3/10

 Cooking Time: 10 minutes

 Servings: 2

INGREDIENTS

- 2 eggplant, sliced
- 1 tbsp. olive oil
- salt and pepper
- cherry tomatoes
- 1 tbsp. mint, chopped
- 1 tsp. red wine vinegar

DESCRIPTION

STEP 1

Coat the eggplant with oil and season with salt and pepper.

STEP 2

Air fry at 400°F for 10-15 minutes or until browned and cooked through.

STEP 3

Top the grilled eggplant with the minty salsa. Serve straight away.

NUTRITIONAL INFORMATION

Calories 71, Fat 5 g, Carbs 6 g, Protein 2 g

DELICIOUS VEGGIE BURGER

Cooking Difficulty: 3/10	Cooking Time: 35 minutes	Servings: 4

INGREDIENTS

- 1 tbsp. olive oil
- salt
- pepper
- 1 ribbed bow
- 1 can canned chickpeas
- 0.5 tsp soy sauce
- 0.5 teaspoon worcester sauce
- 4 burger buns

DESCRIPTION

STEP 1
Place the chickpeas in a blender and blend until smooth. Add soy sauce and worcester sauce to the mixture and mix well.

STEP 2
Form 4 cutlets from the mass. Spray the air fryer grate with olive oil. Carefully place the patties in the basket so they are not touching. Cook for 6 minutes at 400 degrees flipping once carefully at the halfway mark.

STEP 3
Then place them between the hamburger buns and add your favorite vegetables and sauce. Enjoy!

NUTRITIONAL INFORMATION

Calories: 390; Fat: 6.3 g; Carbs: 21.1 g; Protein: 5.6 g

QUINOA AND SPINACH CAKES

Cooking Difficulty: 2/10	Cooking Time: 9 minutes	Servings: 10

INGREDIENTS

- 2 c. cooked quinoa
- 1 c. chopped baby spinach
- 1 egg
- 2 tbsps. minced parsley
- 1 tsp. minced garlic
- 1 carrot, peeled and shredded
- 1 chopped onion
- ¼ c. vegan milk
- 1 c. breadcrumbs
- sea salt
- ground black peppe

DESCRIPTION

STEP 1
In a mixing bowl, mix all ingredients. Season with salt and pepper to taste.

STEP 2
Preheat your Air Fryer to 390°F.

STEP 3
Scoop ¼ cup of quinoa and spinach mixture and place in the Air Fryer cooking basket. Cook in batches until browned for about 8 minutes.

STEP 4
Serve and enjoy!

NUTRITIONAL INFORMATION

Calories: 188, Fat: 4.4 g, Carbs: 31.2g, Protein: 8.1g

CHEESY LEEK & KALE QUICHE

 Cooking Difficulty: 3/10

 Cooking Time: 35 minutes

 Servings: 6

INGREDIENTS

- 1 vegan pie crust (store-bought or homemade)
- 1 tablespoon olive oil
- 2 leeks, thinly sliced
- 2 cups kale, chopped
- 1 cup firm tofu, drained and crumbled
- 1 cup unsweetened plant-based milk
- 1/4 cup nutritional yeast
- 2 tablespoons cornstarch
- 1 teaspoon garlic powder
- 1/2 teaspoon turmeric
- Salt and pepper to taste

NUTRITIONAL INFORMATION

Calories: 178, Fat: 10.1g, Carbs: 9.2g, Protein: 13.4g

DESCRIPTION

STEP 1
Preheat your air fryer to 375°F.

STEP 2
Heat olive oil in a skillet over medium heat. Add the sliced leeks and sauté until they become tender, about 5-7 minutes. Add the chopped kale and cook for an additional 2 minutes until the kale wilts. Remove from heat and set aside.

STEP 3
In a mixing bowl, combine the crumbled tofu, plant-based milk, nutritional yeast, cornstarch, garlic powder, turmeric, salt, and pepper. Stir well until all the ingredients are fully incorporated.

STEP 4
Roll out the vegan pie crust and line a greased air fryer-safe quiche pan or pie dish with it. Trim any excess crust.

STEP 5
Spread the sautéed leeks and kale evenly over the crust. Pour the tofu mixture over the vegetables, making sure it is spread out evenly.

STEP 6
Place the quiche in the air fryer basket and cook for about 25-30 minutes, or until the crust is golden and the filling is set.

STEP 7
Once cooked, remove the quiche from the air fryer and let it cool for a few minutes before slicing and serving.

BAKED CAULIFLOWER

Cooking Difficulty: 2/10	Cooking Time: 15 minutes	Servings: 4

INGREDIENTS

- 2 minced garlic cloves
- 2 tbsps. olive oil
- 1 lb. cauliflower florets
- ½ tsp. ground nutmeg
- ½ tsps. dried rosemary
- ½ tsps. smoked paprika (optional)
- salt
- black pepper

DESCRIPTION

STEP 1
Combine the cauliflower with the garlic and the other ingredients, toss and transfer to air fryer, and set to 375F for 10 minutes. Shake halfway through.

STEP 2
Once the timer goes off, remove it and serve immediately.

NUTRITIONAL INFORMATION

Calories 150, Fat 4.1g, Carbs 3.2g, Protein 2g

BROCCOLI AND TOFU

 Cooking Difficulty: 3/10

 Cooking Time: 20 minutes

 Servings: 2

INGREDIENTS

- 1 head of broccoli
- tofu
- 1 clove of garlic
- 3 tsp soy sauce
- oyster souse (optional)
- salt and pepper

DESCRIPTION

STEP 1

Cut broccoli flowers into small pieces. Wrap the tofu in a paper towel and press lightly to remove excess liquid, then crush with a fork.

STEP 2

Finely chop the garlic, mix with the soy sauce, then add the tofu and stir gently.

STEP 3

Add tofu to air fryer basket, and cook at 375 degrees for 10 minutes. Shake basket, add broccoli, shake again, then cook for another 10-15 minutes at 375. Serve over rice.

NUTRITIONAL INFORMATION

190 Calories, 6g Protein, 7g Fat, 5,4g Carbs

CHICKPEA AND SPINACH CUTLETS

Cooking Difficulty: 3/10	Cooking Time: 40 minutes	Servings: 12

NUTRITIONAL INFORMATION

120 Calories, 3.5g Fats, 20g Net Carbs, and 2g Protein

INGREDIENTS

- 1 red bell pepper
- 19 oz. chickpeas, rinsed & drained
- 1 c. ground almonds
- 2 tsps. dijon mustard
- ½ tsp. sage
- 1 c. spinach, fresh
- 1½ c. rolled oats
- 1 clove garlic, pressed
- ½ lemon, juiced
- 2 tsps. maple syrup, pure

DESCRIPTION

STEP 1

Get out a baking sheet. Line it with parchment paper. Cut your red pepper in half and then take the seeds out. Place it on your baking sheet, and roast in the oven while you prepare your other ingredients.

STEP 2

Process your chickpeas, almonds, mustard, and maple syrup together in a food processor. Add in your lemon juice, sage, garlic, and spinach, processing again. Make sure it's combined, but don't puree it.

STEP 3

Once your red bell pepper is softened, which should roughly take ten minutes, add this to the processor as well. Add in your oats, mixing well.

STEP 4

Form twelve patties. Spray the air fryer grate with olive oil. Carefully place the patties in the basket so they are not touching. You may have to do 2 batches to achieve this. Cook for 16 minutes at 400 degrees flipping once carefully at the halfway mark.

DELICIOUS MUSHROOMS

Cooking Difficulty: 2/10	Cooking Time: 15 minutes	Servings: 3

INGREDIENTS

- 1 pound fresh chanterelle mushrooms, cleaned and trimmed
- 1 large onion, thinly sliced
- 2 tablespoons olive oil
- 1 teaspoon garlic powder
- 1/2 teaspoon smoked paprika
- Salt and pepper to taste
- Fresh parsley or thyme for garnish (optional)

DESCRIPTION

STEP 1
Preheat your air fryer to 400°F. In a mixing bowl all ingredients. Toss well to coat the mushrooms and onions evenly with the seasoning.

STEP 2
Place the seasoned mushrooms and onions in the air fryer basket in a single layer. You may need to cook them in batches depending on the size of your air fryer.

STEP 3
Cook the mushrooms and onions in the air fryer for about 10-12 minutes. Once cooked, remove the mushrooms and onions from the air fryer and transfer them to a serving dish.

NUTRITIONAL INFORMATION

Calories: 120; Fat: 3.3 g; Carbs: 5.1 g; Protein: 5.6 g

CAULIFLOWER PATTIES

 Cooking Difficulty: 3/10

 Cooking Time: 35 minutes

 Servings: 6

INGREDIENTS

- 1 medium head of cauliflower, cut into florets
- 1/2 cup breadcrumbs (you can use gluten-free breadcrumbs if desired)
- 1/4 cup nutritional yeast
- 2 tablespoons ground flaxseed
- 3 tablespoons water
- 2 cloves garlic, minced
- 1 teaspoon onion powder
- 1 teaspoon smoked paprika
- 1/2 teaspoon salt
- 1/4 teaspoon black pepper
- spinach (optional)
- Cooking spray

NUTRITIONAL INFORMATION

278 Calories, 23.9g Fat, 3.4g Carbs, 12.3g Protein

STEP 1
Preheat your air fryer to 375°F.

STEP 2
Place the cauliflower florets in a microwave-safe bowl and cover with a microwave-safe lid or plate. Microwave on high for about 5 minutes, or until the cauliflower is tender. Alternatively, you can steam the cauliflower until tender.

STEP 3
Once the cauliflower is cooked, transfer it to a large mixing bowl and mash it using a fork or potato masher until it reaches a rice-like consistency.

STEP 4
In a small bowl, combine the ground flaxseed and water. Let it sit for a few minutes until it thickens and forms a gel-like consistency.

STEP 5
To the mashed cauliflower, add all other ingredients, and the flaxseed mixture. Mix well until all the ingredients are combined and the mixture holds together.

STEP 6
Shape the mixture into patties using your hands or a cookie cutter. Make sure to compact the mixture firmly so that the patties hold their shape.

STEP 7
Lightly grease the air fryer basket with cooking spray. Place the cauliflower patties in the basket in a single layer, leaving some space between them. Air fry the patties for about 12-15 minutes, flipping them halfway through the cooking time. Serve and enjoy!

SPICE-ROASTED CARROTS

 Cooking Difficulty:
2/10

 Cooking Time:
30 minutes

 Servings:
2

INGREDIENTS

- 8 large carrots
- 3 tbsps. olive oil
- 1 tbsp. red wine vinegar
- 2 tbsps. packed fresh oregano leaves
- ½ tsp. ground nutmeg
- 1 tbsps. vegan butter
- ⅓ c. salted pistachios, roasted
- salt and pepper

DESCRIPTION

STEP 1
Mix oregano, oil, nutmeg, carrots, salt, and pepper in a roasting pan.

STEP 2
Turn your air fryer to 360 degrees F and cook for 15-18 minutes, shaking the basket after 7 minutes.

STEP 3
Transfer to a plate.

STEP 4
Top with vinegar, butter, and top with pistachios before serving.

NUTRITIONAL INFORMATION

120 Calories, 3.5g Fats, 20g Net Carbs, and 2g Protein

AIR FRIED TOFU WITH PEANUT DIPPING SAUCE

Cooking Difficulty: 3/10	Cooking Time: 10 minutes	Servings: 6

NUTRITIONAL INFORMATION

Calories: 256, Fat: 14.1g, Carbs: 21.2g, Protein: 12.4 g.

INGREDIENTS

- 16 oz. cubed firm tofu
- 185g all-purpose flour
- ½ tsp. salt
- ½ tsp. ground black pepper
- olive oil spray
  For the dipping sauce:
- 1/3 c. smooth low-sodium peanut butter
- 1 tsp. minced garlic
- 2 tbsps. light soy sauce
- 1 tbsp. fresh lime juice
- 1 tsp. sugar
- 1/3 c. water
- 2 tbsps. chopped roasted

DESCRIPTION

STEP 1
In a bowl, mix all dipping sauce ingredients. Cover it with plastic wrap and keep refrigerated until ready to serve.

STEP 2
To make the fried tofu, season all-purpose flour with salt and pepper.

STEP 3
Coat the tofu cubes with the flour mixture. Spray with oil.

STEP 4
Preheat your Air Fryer to 390°F.

STEP 5
Place coated tofu in the cooking basket. Careful not to overcrowd them.

STEP 6
Cook until browned for approximately 8 minutes.

STEP 7
Serve with prepared peanut dipping sauce. Enjoy!

ONION TARTS

 Cooking Difficulty: 3/10	Cooking Time: 25 minutes	Servings: 6

INGREDIENTS

- 1 sheet of vegan puff pastry, thawed
- vegan cheese (optional)
- 2 large onions, thinly sliced
- 2 tablespoons olive oil
- 1 tablespoon balsamic vinegar
- 1 teaspoon sugar
- Salt and pepper to taste
- Fresh thyme leaves for garnish (optional)

NUTRITIONAL INFORMATION

Calories 389, Fat 24.9g, Carbs 30.21g, Protein 12g

DESCRIPTION

STEP 1
Preheat your air fryer to 375°F.

STEP 2
In a skillet, heat the olive oil over medium heat. Add the sliced onions and cook until they become soft and caramelized, stirring occasionally. This process may take about 15-20 minutes.

STEP 3
Once the onions are caramelized, add the balsamic vinegar, sugar, salt, and pepper. Stir well to combine and cook for another 2-3 minutes. Remove from heat and let it cool slightly.

STEP 4
Roll out the vegan puff pastry sheet on a lightly floured surface. Cut the pastry into smaller squares or rectangles, depending on the size you prefer for your tarts.

STEP 5
Place a spoonful of the caramelized onions onto each piece of puff pastry, leaving a small border around the edges. Add vegan grated cheese on top if desired.

STEP 6
Transfer the tarts to the air fryer basket, leaving some space between them. Cook in the air fryer for about 10-12 minutes, or until the puff pastry turns golden brown and crispy.

STEP 7
Once cooked, remove the tarts from the air fryer and let them cool for a few minutes. Garnish with fresh thyme leaves if desired.

CAULIFLOWER SALAD

 Cooking Difficulty: 2/10	 Cooking Time: 16 minutes	Servings: 4

INGREDIENTS

- 2 minced garlic cloves
- 2 tbsps. olive oil
- 1 lb. cauliflower florets
- ½ tsps. dried rosemary
- salt
- black pepper
- pomegranate seeds
- coriander leaves
- canned chickpeas

DESCRIPTION

STEP 1
Combine the cauliflower with the garlic and other spices, toss and transfer to air fryer, and set to 375F for 10 minutes. Shake halfway through.

STEP 2
After the timer sounds, mix the cauliflower with the pomegranate, cilantro leaves, and chickpea. Serve the salad and enjoy.

NUTRITIONAL INFORMATION

Calories 95, Fat 3 g, Carbs 4 g, Protein 2 g

BLACK BEAN STUFFED SWEET POTATOES

Cooking Difficulty: 4/10	Cooking Time: 65 minutes	Servings: 4

NUTRITIONAL INFORMATION

Calories: 387, Fat: 16.1 g, Carbs: 53 g, Protein: 10.4 g

INGREDIENTS

- 4 sweet potatoes
- 15 oz. cooked black beans
- ½ tsp. ground black pepper
- ½ red onion, peeled, diced
- ½ tsp. salt
- ¼ tsp. onion powder
- ¼ tsp. garlic powder
- ¼ tsp. red chili powder
- 1 tsp. lime juice
- 1 ½ tbsps. olive oil
- ½ c. cashew cream sauce

DESCRIPTION

STEP 1
Scrub and dry the potatoes, then poke them with a fork. Air fry sweet potatoes at 370 degrees F for 40 to 50 minutes.

STEP 2
Meanwhile, prepare the sauce, and for this, whisk together the cream sauce, black pepper, and lime juice until combined, set aside until required.

STEP 3
When 10 minutes of the baking time of potatoes are left, heat a skillet pan with oil. Add in onion to cook until golden for 5 minutes.

STEP 4
Then stir in spice, cook for another 3 minutes, stir in bean until combined and cook for 5 minutes until hot.

STEP 5
Let roasted sweet potatoes cool for 10 minutes, then cut them open, mash the flesh and top with bean mixture, cilantro and avocado, and then drizzle with cream sauce. Serve straight away.

GREEN BEANS AND POTATOES

 Cooking Difficulty: 1/10

 Cooking Time: 19 minutes

 Servings: 4

INGREDIENTS

- 1 pound green beans, trimmed
- 1 pound baby potatoes, halved
- 2 tablespoons olive oil
- 1 teaspoon garlic powder
- 1 teaspoon dried thyme
- 1 teaspoon dried rosemary
- 1/2 teaspoon salt
- 1/4 teaspoon black pepper
- cooking spray

DESCRIPTION

STEP 1
Preheat the air fryer to 375°F for 5 minutes. In a mixing bowl, toss the green beans and potatoes with olive oil, garlic powder, thyme,rosemar ,salt, and black pepper until evenly coated.

STEP 2
Spray the air fryer basket with cooking spray. Add the green beans and potatoes to the air fryer basket in a single layer.

STEP 3
Cook for 12-15 minutes, shaking the basket every 5 minutes until the green beans and potatoes are tender and lightly browned. Serve.

NUTRITIONAL INFORMATION
Calories 212, Fat 5g, Carbs 34g, Protein 5g

SPAGHETTI WITH ROASTED VEGETABLES

 Cooking Difficulty: 4/10

 Cooking Time: 24 minutes

 Servings: 4

INGREDIENTS

- 10 oz. spaghetti, cooked
- 1 eggplant, chopped
- 1 chopped bell pepper
- 1 zucchini, chopped
- 4 oz. halved grape tomatoes
- 1 tsp. minced garlic
- 4 tbsps. divided olive oil
- salt
- ground black pepper
- 12 oz. can diced tomatoes
- ½ tsp. dried oregano
- 1 tsp. paprika

NUTRITIONAL INFORMATION

Calories: 330, Fat: 12.4g, Carbs: 45.3g, Protein: 9.9g

DESCRIPTION

STEP 1
In a mixing bowl, combine together eggplant, red bell pepper, zucchini, grape tomatoes, garlic, and 2 tablespoons olive oil. Add some salt and pepper, to taste.

STEP 2
Preheat your Air Fryer to 390°F.

STEP 3
Place vegetable mixture in the Air Fryer cooking basket and cook for about 10-12 minutes, or until vegetables are tender.

STEP 4
Meanwhile, you can start preparing the tomato sauce.

STEP 5
In a saucepan, heat remaining 2 tablespoons olive oil. Stir fry garlic for 2 minutes. Add diced tomatoes and simmer for 3 minutes.

STEP 6
Stir in oregano, paprika. Season with salt and pepper, to taste. Let it cook for another 5-7 minutes.

STEP 7
Once cooked, transfer the vegetables from Air Fryer to a mixing bowl.

STEP 8
Add the cooked spaghetti and prepared a sauce. Toss to combine well.

STEP 9
Divide among 4 serving plates. Serve and enjoy!

ASPARAGUS WITH LEMON

 Cooking Difficulty: 1/10

 Cooking Time: 12 minutes

 Servings: 1

INGREDIENTS

- 1 bunch of asparagus
- 1 tablespoon olive oil
- 1 lemon
- Salt and pepper to taste

DESCRIPTION

STEP 1
Preheat the fryer to 400°F (200°C).

STEP 2
Wash the asparagus and trim off the tough ends. Put the trimmed asparagus spears in a bowl and drizzle with olive oil. Add lemon juice, salt, and pepper, and mix well.

STEP 3
Place the seasoned asparagus in the basket of the fryer. Cook the asparagus in the air fryer for about 8-10 minutes, or until tender and lightly browned. When the asparagus is cooked, remove it from the fryer and transfer it to a serving dish.

NUTRITIONAL INFORMATION
110 Calories, 4g Protein, 3g Fat, 5g Carbs

BAKED BROCCOLI

 Cooking Difficulty: 2/10

 Cooking Time: 10 minutes

 Servings: 4

INGREDIENTS

- 2 minced garlic cloves
- 2 tbsps. olive oil
- 1 lb. broccoli florets
- ½ tsp. ground nutmeg
- black pepper

DESCRIPTION

STEP 1
Combine the broccoli with the garlic and the other ingredients, toss and transfer to air fryer, and set to 375F for 8 minutes. Shake halfway through.

STEP 2
Once the timer goes off, remove it and serve immediately.

NUTRITIONAL INFORMATION

Calories 150, Fat 4.1g, Carbs 3.2g, Protein 2g

ZUCCHINI CAKES

 Cooking Difficulty: 2/10	Cooking Time: 22 minutes	Servings: 4

INGREDIENTS

- 2 tbsps. olive oil
- 2 tbsps. almond flour
- 1/3 c. carrot, shredded
- 1 tsp. lemon zest, grated
- 1 garlic clove, minced
- 1 egg, whisked
- 2 zucchinis, grated
- 1 yellow onion, chopped
- black pepper
- sea salt

DESCRIPTION

STEP 1
In a bowl, combine the zucchinis with the garlic, onion, and the other ingredients except for the oil, stir well and shape medium cakes out of this mix.

STEP 2
Air fry at 375 degrees F for 15 minutes, flipping them over at the 10-minute mark, divide between plates and serve with a side salad.

NUTRITIONAL INFORMATION

Calories 271, Fat 8.7g, Carbs 14.3g, Protein 4.6g

CAULIFLOWER STEAK

 Cooking Difficulty: 2/10	Cooking Time: 27 minutes	Servings: 2

INGREDIENTS

- 2 heads cauliflower
- 1 tsp. olive oil
- ¼ tsp. smoked paprika
- 1 tsp. coriander
- ¼ tsp. black pepper

DESCRIPTION

STEP 1
Remove the bottom core of the cauliflower. Stand it on its base, starting in the middle, and slice it in half. Then slice steaks about ¾ inches thick.

STEP 2
Using olive oil, coat the front and back of the steaks. Sprinkle with coriander, paprika, and pepper.

STEP 3
Place the cauliflower steaks in the air fryer basket, and cook in the air fryer at 375 F for 15 minutes. Gently flip the steak halfway through and season again. Keep cooking until desire doneness. Serve with your favorite sauce.

NUTRITIONAL INFORMATION
Calories 234, Fat 3.8g, Carbs 40.3g, Protein 14.5g

GRILLED CORN

 Cooking Difficulty: 1/10

 Cooking Time: 17 minutes

 Servings: 2

INGREDIENTS

- 4 ears of corn, peeled
- 2 tablespoons olive oil
- 1/2 tsp. garlic powder
- 1/4 tsp. salt
- cooking spray
  for the sauce:
- 2 cloves garlic
- olive oil
- parsley

DESCRIPTION

STEP 1

Preheat a deep fryer to 375°F. In a small bowl, mix together the olive oil and corn spices. Using a brush, apply the oil mixture to the corn cobs. Spray a deep fryer basket with cooking spray and place the corn in it.

STEP 2

Cook the corn in the air fryer for 10-12 minutes. Meanwhile, make the sauce. Chop parsley leaves and garlic cloves and mix with olive oil.

STEP 3

When the corn is ready, remove it from the air fryer and transfer it to a serving platter. Serve with the sauce.

NUTRITIONAL INFORMATION

165 Calories, 2g Fat, 1.5g Carbs, 3g Protein

CHILI PARSNIP

 Cooking Difficulty: 2/10	Cooking Time: 20 minutes	Servings: 4

NUTRITIONAL INFORMATION

Calories 83, Fat 3.7g, Carbs 12.22g, Protein 2g

INGREDIENTS

- 1 pound parsnips, peeled and sliced into fries
- 2 tablespoons olive oil
- 1 teaspoon chili powder
- 1/2 teaspoon onion powder
- 1/2 teaspoon salt
- 1/4 teaspoon black pepper

DESCRIPTION

STEP 1
Preheat the air fryer to 375°F.

STEP 2
In a mixing bowl, toss the parsnips with olive oil until coated.

STEP 3
Add chili powder, onionpowder, salt, and pepper to the bowl and mix well.

STEP 4
Place the parsnips in the air fryer basket, making sure they are in a single layer.

STEP 5
Cook the parsnips for 12-15 minutes or until they are crispy and golden brown, shaking the basket halfway through the cooking time to ensure even cooking.

STEP 6
Remove the parsnips from the air fryer basket and transfer to a serving plate.

STEP 7
Serve hot and enjoy!

GRILLED ZUCCHINI RINGS

 Cooking Difficulty: 2/10

 Cooking Time: 16 minutes

 Servings: 2

INGREDIENTS

- 2 medium zucchini
- 1 tsp garlic powder
- 1 tsp onion powder
- 1/2 tsp salt
- 1/4 tsp black pepper
- 2 tbsp olive oil
- cooking spray

DESCRIPTION

STEP 1
Preheat the deep fryer to 375°F. Slice zucchini into 1/4 inch thick slices. In a small bowl, mix olive oil and all the spices. Brush each zucchini circle with olive oil, trying to coat evenly.

STEP 2
Spray a deep fryer basket with cooking spray. Place the zucchini rounds in the deep fryer basket. Cook zucchini in air fryer for 8-10 minutes.

STEP 3
When the zucchini are cooked, remove them from the fryer and transfer them to a serving platter. Serve the grilled zucchini immediately with your favorite sauce or seasoning. Bon appetit!

NUTRITIONAL INFORMATION

Calories: 118, Fat: 10 g, Carbs: 6 g, Protein: 2 g

CAULIFLOWER STEAK IN BBQ SAUCE

 Cooking Difficulty: 2/10

 Cooking Time: 18 minutes

 Servings: 6

INGREDIENTS

- 1 head of cauliflower
- 2 tbsp olive oil
- 1 tsp onion powder
- salt and pepper to taste
- 1/4 cup BBQ sauce
- 1 tbsp chopped fresh

NUTRITIONAL INFORMATION

Calories: 110, Fat: 6 g, Carbs: 12 g, Protein: 3 g

STEP 1

Preheat the air fryer to 375°F. Remove the leaves from the cauliflower and cut it into 1-inch thick slices, so that you have cauliflower «steaks.»

STEP 2

In a small bowl, mix together the olive oil, onion powder, salt, and pepper.

STEP 3

Brush each cauliflower steak with the oil mixture, making sure to coat it evenly.

STEP 4

Place the cauliflower steaks in the air fryer basket, making sure to leave some space between each piece.

STEP 5

Cook the cauliflower in the air fryer for 12-15 minutes, flipping the steaks halfway through the cooking time, or until they are tender and golden brown.

STEP 6

While the cauliflower is cooking, heat the BBQ sauce in a small saucepan over medium heat until it starts to bubble.

STEP 7

Once the cauliflower is cooked, remove it from the air fryer and place it on a serving platter.

STEP 8

Drizzle the hot BBQ sauce over the cauliflower steaks, making sure to cover them evenly. Serve the grilled cauliflower steaks immediately with your favorite side dish. Enjoy!

BBQ GRILLED CORN

 Cooking Difficulty: 1/10	 Cooking Time: 17 minutes	Servings: 2

INGREDIENTS

- 4 ears of corn, peeled
- 1 tbsp olive oil
- 1 tsp garlic powder
- 1/4 cup BBQ sauce
- salt and pepper to taste
- cooking spray
- vegan cheese

DESCRIPTION

STEP 1

Preheat a deep fryer to 375°F. In a small bowl, mix olive oil and spices. Using a brush, spread the oil mixture over the corn cobs. Spray a deep fryer basket with cooking spray and place the corn in it.

STEP 2

Cook the corn in the deep fryer for 8 minutes. After that, brush the corn cobs with BBQ sauce and cook for another 4-6 minutes, until nicely crusted.

STEP 3

When the corn is ready, remove it from the fryer and transfer it to a serving platter. Serve on top garnished with vegan cheese.

NUTRITIONAL INFORMATION

180 Calories, 4g Fat, 2.5g Carbs, 3g Protein

APPETIZING BRUSSEL SPROUTS

 Cooking Difficulty: 1/10

 Cooking Time: 17 minutes

 Servings: 4

INGREDIENTS

- 1 pound Brussels sprouts, trimmed and halved
- 2 tablespoons avocado oil
- 1 teaspoon garlic powder
- 1/2 teaspoon salt
- 1/4 teaspoon black pepper

DESCRIPTION

STEP 1

Preheat a deep fryer to 375°F. In a bowl, mix together the avocado oil and all the spices. Add the brussel sprouts to the bowl and mix well.

STEP 2

Place the Brussels sprouts in the fryer basket, making sure they lie in a single layer.

STEP 3

Cook the brussels sprouts for 12-15 minutes or until crispy on the outside and tender on the inside. Serve with your favorite sauce.

NUTRITIONAL INFORMATION

110 Calories, 4 g Fat, 4g Carbs, 2g Protein

PERFECT BRUSSELS SPROUT AND CHEESE

Cooking Difficulty: 2/10	Cooking Time: 22 minutes	Servings: 2

INGREDIENTS

- ¾ c. brussels sprouts
- 1 tbsp. extra virgin olive oil
- 1 teaspoon garlic powder
- ¼ tsp. salt
- freshly ground black pepper
- ¼ c. grated mozzarella cheese

NUTRITIONAL INFORMATION

Calories: 224, Fat: 18.1g, Protein: 10.1g, Carbs: 4.5g

STEP 1

Cut the Brussels sprouts into halves then place in a bowl.

STEP 2

Drizzle extra virgin olive oil over the Brussels sprouts then sprinkle salt on top. Toss to combine.

STEP 3

Preheat an Air Fryer to 375°F (191°C).

STEP 4

Transfer the seasoned Brussels sprouts to the Air Fryer then cook for 15 minutes.

STEP 5

After 15 minutes, open the Air Fryer and sprinkle grated Mozzarella cheese over the cooked Brussels sprouts.

STEP 6

Cook the Brussels sprouts in the Air Fryer for 5 minutes or until the Mozzarella cheese is melted.

STEP 7

Once it is done, remove from the Air Fryer then transfer to a serving dish.

STEP 8

Serve and enjoy.

BAKED POTATO

 Cooking Difficulty: 1/10	 Cooking Time: 19 minutes	Servings: 2

INGREDIENTS

- 2-3 medium-sized potatoes
- 1-2 tablespoons olive oil
- Salt and pepper to taste
- Optional seasonings: garlic powder, paprika, rosemary, or any other herbs and spices you prefer

DESCRIPTION

STEP 1
Start by preheating the fryer to 400°F. Wash the potatoes thoroughly and cut them in half and then cut each half into 3 pieces.

STEP 2
Mix the olive oil with the salt and the rest of the spices of your choice, add the potatoes, and mix thoroughly. Arrange the potato slices in the basket of the deep fryer in a single layer. Cook for 10-15 minutes, turning it halfway through the cooking time.

STEP 3
After cooking, transfer the potato slices to a plate lined with a paper towel to soak up the excess oil. Allow them to cool slightly before serving.

NUTRITIONAL INFORMATION

Calories: 147, Fat: 3.7g, Carbs: 26.7g, Protein: 3g

SNACKS & DESSERTS

FRIED GREEN BEANS GARLIC

 Cooking Difficulty: 2/10

 Cooking Time: 5 minutes

 Servings: 2

INGREDIENTS

- ¾ c. chopped green beans
- 3 tsps. minced garlic
- 2 tbsps. rosemary
- ½ tsp. salt
- 1 tbsp. vegan butter

DESCRIPTION

STEP 1
Preheat an Air Fryer to 390°F.

STEP 2
Place the chopped green beans in the Air Fryer then brush with butter.

STEP 3
Sprinkle salt, minced garlic, and rosemary over the green beans then cook for 5 minutes.

STEP 4
Once the green beans are done, remove from the Air Fryer then place on a serving dish. Serve and enjoy warm.

NUTRITIONAL INFORMATION

Calories: 72, Fat: 6.3g, Protein: 0.7g, Carbs: 4.5g

CAULIFLOWER POPCORN

 Cooking Difficulty: 2/10

 Cooking Time: 17 minutes

 Servings: 6

INGREDIENTS

- 1 head of cauliflower
- 1/4 cup all-purpose flour
- 1/2 tsp garlic powder
- 1/2 tsp onion powder
- 1/2 tsp paprika
- 1/2 tsp salt
- 1/4 tsp black pepper
- 1/4 cup unsweetened vegan milk

NUTRITIONAL INFORMATION

Calories 150, Fat 4.1g, Carbs 3.2g, Protein 2g

DESCRIPTION

STEP 1
Preheat the air fryer to 400°F.

STEP 2
Cut the cauliflower into bite-sized florets.

STEP 3
In a small bowl, mix together the flour, garlic powder, onion powder, paprika, salt, and black pepper.

STEP 4
Pour the almond milk into another small bowl.

STEP 5
Dip each cauliflower floret in the almond milk, making sure it is coated evenly, and roll the cauliflower floret in the flour mixture.

STEP 6
Spray the air fryer basket with cooking spray. Place the cauliflower florets in the air fryer basket, making sure to leave some space between each piece.

STEP 7
Cook the cauliflower in the air fryer for 10-12 minutes, shaking the basket halfway through the cooking time, or until they are crispy and golden brown.

STEP 8
Once the cauliflower is cooked, remove it from the air fryer and place it on a serving platter.

STEP 9
Serve the cauliflower popcorn immediately with your favorite dipping sauce or seasoning. Enjoy!

PEACH WITH CINNAMON DESSERT

 Cooking Difficulty: 2/10	Cooking Time: 7 minutes	Servings: 2

INGREDIENTS

- 2 ripe peaches, stoned and quartered
- 0,5 tbsp. lemon juice
- 1 tsp. cinnamon powder

DESCRIPTION

STEP 1
Preheat Air Fryer to 360°F.

STEP 2
Coat all peaches with cinnamon powder.

STEP 3
Place the peaches in the Air Fryer cooking basket and cook for 5-7 minutes.

STEP 4
Transfer into a serving dish. Drizzle with lemon juice. Serve and enjoy!

NUTRITIONAL INFORMATION

Calories: 72, Fat: 6.3g, Protein: 0.7g, Carbs: 4.5g

GLAZED PEARS

Cooking Difficulty: 2/10	Cooking Time: 17 minutes	Servings: 2

NUTRITIONAL INFORMATION

Calories: 241; Fat: 0.7g; Carbs: 60.4g; Protein: 3g

INGREDIENTS

- 2 ripe pears, peeled and sliced in half
- 2 tablespoons unsalted vegan butter, melted
- 1 tablespoon honey
- 1/2 teaspoon ground cinnamon

DESCRIPTION

STEP 1
Preheat the air fryer to 375°F.

STEP 2
In a mixing bowl, whisk together melted butter, honey, and cinnamon.

STEP 3
Add the sliced pears to the bowl and toss to coat with the glaze.

STEP 4
Place the pears in the air fryer basket, making sure they are in a single layer.

STEP 5
Cook the pears for 8-10 minutes, shaking the basket halfway through the cooking time to ensure even cooking.

STEP 6
Remove the pears from the air fryer basket and transfer to a serving plate.

STEP 7
Serve hot and enjoy.

CELERY & CARROT SIDE DISH

 Cooking Difficulty: 1/10

 Cooking Time: 15 minutes

 Servings: 4

INGREDIENTS

- 2 cups celery, sliced
- 2 cups carrots, sliced
- 2 tablespoons olive oil
- 1/2 teaspoon garlic powder
- 1/2 teaspoon onion powder
- 1/2 teaspoon salt
- 1/4 teaspoon black pepper

DESCRIPTION

STEP 1
Preheat a deep fryer to 375°F. In a mixing bowl, add celery and carrots with olive oil and all spices. Mix well.

STEP 2
Place the vegetables in the basket of the air fryer, making sure they are in a single layer. Cook the vegetables for 10-12 minutes or until they are tender and lightly browned.

STEP 3
Remove the vegetables from the air fryer basket and transfer to a serving platter. Serve hot and enjoy.

NUTRITIONAL INFORMATION

100 Calories, 3g Fat, 8g Carbs, 3g Protein

MINTY PUMPKIN CHEESE BOMBS

 Cooking Difficulty: 4/10

 Cooking Time: 27 minutes

 Servings: 4

INGREDIENTS

- ¾ lb. pumpkin
- ¼ c. chopped onion
- ¼ c. chopped parsley
- 2 tsps. chopped mint leaves
- ¼ c. almond flour
- 2 tbsps. vegan butter
- 1 tsp. thyme
- 1½ tbsp. mustard
- ½ tsp. salt
- ½ tsp. pepper
- ¼ lb. mozzarella cheese
- 1 egg
- 1 c. roasted pecans

NUTRITIONAL INFORMATION

Calories 150, Fat 4.1g, Carbs 3.2g, Protein 2g

STEP 1

Peel the pumpkin then cut into cubes. Place the cubed pumpkin in a food processor then process until smooth.

STEP 2

Transfer the smooth pumpkin to a bowl then add chopped onion, parsley, mint leaves, and flour. Pour melted butter into the bowl then season with thyme, mustard, salt, and pepper. Mix until combined.

STEP 3

Shape the pumpkin mixture into small balls the fill each ball with Mozzarella cheese. Arrange the pumpkin balls on a tray then refrigerate for 15 minutes.

STEP 4

Meanwhile, place the roasted pecans in a food processor then process until smooth and becoming crumbles. Set aside.

STEP 5

In a separate bowl, crack the egg then using a fork stir until incorporated.

STEP 6

Preheat an Air Fryer to 400°F (204°C).

STEP 7

Take the pumpkin bowl out of the refrigerator then dip in the egg. Roll the pumpkin balls in the pecan crumbles then arrange on the Air Fryer's rack.

STEP 8

Cook the pumpkin balls for 12 minutes then remove from heat. Serve and enjoy warm.

BRUSCHETTA WITH PESTO CHEESE AND TOMATO

Cooking Difficulty: 2/10	Cooking Time: 6 minutes	Servings: 6

INGREDIENTS

- 1 loaf baguette, sliced crosswise into 12 slices
- 1 c. sliced cherry tomatoes
- 4 oz. mozzarella cheese, shredded
- ¾ c. prepared pesto
- ¼ c. parsley leaves, coarsely chopped (optional)

DESCRIPTION

STEP 1
Preheat Air Fryer to 390°F.

STEP 2
To one side of baguette, spread pesto sauce and top with mozzarella and then with sliced cherry tomatoes.

STEP 3
Place bruschetta in the Air Fryer cooking basket and cook for 3-5 minutes. Sprinkle with fresh parsley.

STEP 4
Transfer bruschetta into a serving dish. Serve and enjoy!

NUTRITIONAL INFORMATION

Calories: 216, Fat: 8.2g, Carbs: 27g, Protein: 9g

SWEET POTATO FRIES WITH BASIL

Cooking Difficulty: 2/10	Cooking Time: 25 minutes	Servings: 6

INGREDIENTS

- 6 sweet potatoes, sliced
- ¼ c. olive oil
- 2 tbsps. chopped basil leaves, fresh
- 1/2 teaspoon ground cinnamon
- 5g sweet paprika
- ½ tsp. sea salt
- ½ tsp. black pepper

DESCRIPTION

STEP 1
Soak the sweet potatoes in water for at least 30 minutes. Drain thoroughly and pat dry with paper towel.

STEP 2
Preheat your Air Fryer to 360°F. Combine the olive oil, basil, paprika, cinnamon, salt, and pepper in a large bowl. Add the sliced sweet potatoes. Toss to coat well.

STEP 3
Transfer the sweet potatoes into the cooking basket and cook until browned for about 25 minutes. Garnish with basil leaves. Serve and enjoy!

NUTRITIONAL INFORMATION

Calories: 438, Fat: 41.3g, Protein: 12g, Carbs: 9.9g

CONCLUSION

I sincerely hope that you have enjoyed reading this recipe book as much as I have enjoyed writing it. I am confident that my recipe collection will offer you some new and healthy options to add to your daily diet. The best thing that I discovered while writing this book is that your meals do not have to be tasteless and boring to be healthy. I wish you immense success in adding new and healthier meal choices to your diet—that is not only good for you but taste delightful!

Henry Irving

Made in the USA
Las Vegas, NV
07 December 2023

82294587R00083